Puffin Books

Limerick Delight

The limerick has been one of the most popular verse-forms in our language for over 150 years. Here E. O. Parrott has collected together over three hundred hilarious limericks especially for children – from Lear to Milligan, old favourites and new. Pick a subject from this treasury of wit; from *Silly People* and *Sad Ends* to *Curious Tales* and *Twists of the Tongue* – there's something for everybody.

Interspersed with zany illustrations, this riotous concoction of quirky, clever and curious verses will certainly delight and amaze all who discover it.

Varun doesn't like homework,
  That's something he'd rather shirk,
His teachers think it's too bad,
  His parents are a little sad,
But to him it makes no 차이 /

Mama .

Limerick Delight

Chosen by

E. O. Parrott

Illustrated by

David Simonds

PUFFIN BOOKS

Puffin Books, Penguin Books Ltd, Harmondsworth, Middlesex, England
Viking Penguin Inc., 40 West 23rd Street, New York, New York 10010, U.S.A.
Penguin Books Australia Ltd, Ringwood, Victoria, Australia
Penguin Books Canada Limited, 2801 John Street, Markham, Ontario,
Canada L3R 1B4
Penguin Books (N.Z.) Ltd, 182–190 Wairau Road, Auckland 10, New Zealand

First published 1985
Reprinted 1985

This collection copyright © E. O. Parrott, 1985
Illustrations copyright © David Simonds, 1985
All rights reserved

Printed and bound in Great Britain by
Cox & Wyman Ltd, Reading
Set in Linotron Sabon by
Rowland Phototypesetting Ltd,
Bury St Edmunds, Suffolk

Contents

If you look very hard at the STUFF IN
This book, which is known as a PUFFIN,
    You'll very soon know it's
    Been written by poets
For money, of course, not for NUFFIN.

Anon.

There was this lad called Varun
whose parents thought he'd be a boon,
    But he refuses to eat,
    Dal- Bhaat Rotti & sweet,
Now they force feed him with a spoon
— Mama —

Introduction

All the world loves a limerick. Well, no, not quite, but it's certainly true that for over a hundred and fifty years it has been one of the most popular forms of verse in our language. Just why this should be so is not easy to explain. Perhaps its catchy rhythm and simple rhyming pattern give the limerick its wide appeal. Certainly the American humorist, D. McCord, seems to think so:

> Well, it's partly the shape of the thing
> That gives the old Limerick wing;
> Those accordion pleats,
> Full of airy conceits,
> Take it up like a kite on a string.

Although the verse form had been used by poets in various ways for hundreds of years, the first 'true' limericks seem to have appeared in a book of nonsense verse for children (*The History of Sixteen Wonderful Old Women*, published anonymously in 1820). Two years later, a second, similar book appeared (*Anecdotes and Adventures of Fifteen Gentlemen*). Both became very popular with children of the period.

A few years later, Edward Lear imitated these verses in his *Book of Nonsense*, which he wrote for the children of his employer, the Earl of Derby. Here is one of the most famous of his nonsense verses:

There was an Old Man of Thermopylae,
Who never did anything properly;
    But they said: 'If you choose
    To cook eggs in your shoes,
You shall never return to Thermopylae.'

Many people now find Lear's last lines repetitive and tame, but we must remember that each verse was accompanied by a very funny illustration, and we really need to see them together to appreciate the humour of the situation. Lear was an artist by profession, not a writer. Nowadays, however, we demand a much sharper, wittier last line; we want a surprise ending, a 'twist in the tail'.

Some limericks depend for their humour upon the quirks and oddities of English spelling and pronunciation. In this next limerick, the anonymous author is really saying that if we pronounce 'Thames' as if it were spelt 'Tems', then it might be fun to spell words which rhyme with 'Thames' in the same illogical way:

A lady who lived by the Thames
Had a gorgeous collection of ghames;
    She had them re-set
    In a large coronet,
And a number of small diadhames.

Similarly, Mark Twain wittily argues that since 'Co.' stands for 'Company', then phrases that rhyme with 'Company' can be abbreviated in the same way:

A man from John Smith and Co.
Loudly declared he would tho.
    Man that he saw
    Dumping dirt near his door;
The drivers, therefore, didn't do.

Some limericks of this type may be rather baffling if you do not understand a particular abbreviation or correct pronunciation. So far as this book is concerned, you will find a glossary of pronunciations and abbreviations at the end.

Edward Lear never referred to his verses as 'limericks', and, in fact, the word did not appear in any dictionary until 1892, a few years after he had died.

There are a number of different theories as to why this particular verse form should have been given the name of an Irish town. It has been pointed out that, in the eighteenth century, a group of Irish poets, meeting in taverns, wrote light-hearted verses of this type. However, the name may not have been derived from the town itself, but may come from the words '*laoi meidhreach*', which is Irish for 'a merry lay' (song). Whatever the origin of the name, it is fairly certain that translations of these verses became known in England soon after Edward Lear and his anonymous predecessors began publishing their own nonsense verses in the same form, and that finally, because of their similarity, the Irish name for them became attached to both groups of verses.

All sorts of other reasons have been suggested, but I don't think it matters very much! It is probably better not to worry about such things, but just enjoy the limericks.

I hope you will enjoy reading the three hundred or so limericks in this collection, finding your old favourites and some new ones as well. I hope, also, that you will go on to write some of your own, and there is space at the end of this book for your verses and any others that you may come across. I might even be able to include some of them in another anthology one day.

E. O. PARROTT

A Difficult Beginning

There was a young poet of Damn!
There was a young poet of Pembroke,
Who said 'Damn!' whenever Damn!
There was a young poet of Pembroke,
Who said 'Damn!' whenever his pen broke;
    So he'd get a new pen,
    Start all over a Damn!
There was a young poet of Pembroke,
Who said 'Damn!' whenever his pen broke;
    So he'd get a new pen,
    Start all over again,
That determined young poet of DAMN!

William Bealby-Wright

A Spot of Nonsense

Here is Edward Lear, and some friends,
With verse with nonsensical ends;
*   Here's no atom of meaning*
*   That's really worth gleaning,*
But our laughter makes final amends.

There was an Old Man of Berlin,
Whose form was uncommonly thin,
    Till he once, by mistake,
    Was mixed up in a cake,
So they baked the Old Man of Berlin.

Edward Lear

There was an Old Person of Bradley,
Who sang all so loudly and sadly;
    With a poker and tongs,
    He beat time to his songs,
That melodious Old Person of Bradley.

Edward Lear

There was an Old Person of Burton,
Whose answers were rather uncertain;
    When they said: 'How d'ye do?',
    He replied: 'Who are you?',
That distressing Old Person of Burton.

Edward Lear

There was an Old Lady of France,
Who taught little Ducklings to dance;
    When she said: 'Tick-a-tack!',
    They only said: 'Quack!',
Which grieved that Old Lady of France.

Edward Lear

There was an Old Person of Pinner,
As thin as a lath, if not thinner;
    They dressed him in white,
    And rolled him up tight,
That elastic Old Person of Pinner.

Edward Lear

There was a young lady of Lynn,
Who was so uncommonly thin,
    That when she essayed
    To drink lemonade,
She slipped through the straw, and fell in.

Anon.

There was a young fellow called Green,
Whose musical sense wasn't keen;
    He said: 'It is odd,
    But I cannot tell "God
Save the Weasel" from "Pop Goes the Queen!"'

Anon.

There was an old lady of Crewe,
Who set up a home in a shoe;
    There was such a strong pong
    That she moved to Hong Kong,
And now she is doing Kung Fu.

Rachel Moore

A chappie who came from New York,
Tried to teach a parrot to talk;
    But, what a curse!
    It worked in reverse;
Now he goes around saying 'Squawk!'

Spike Milligan

There was an Old Person of Chester,
Whom several small children did pester;
    They threw some large stones,
    Which broke most of his bones,
And displeased that Old Person of Chester.

Edward Lear

There was an Old Man of Peru,
Who watched his wife making a stew;
    But one day by mistake,
    In the stove she did bake
That unfortunate Man of Peru.

Edward Lear

There was a wild youngster of Wembley,
Whose conduct made people feel trembly;
    He released some mad bees
    At a meeting – and these
Caused panic among the assembly.

Langford Reed

There was an Old Man in a Tree,
Whose whiskers were lovely to see,
    But the birds of the air
    Plucked them perfectly bare,
And made themselves nests in the tree.

Edward Lear

There was an Old Man with a Beard,
Who said: 'It is just as I feared.
    Two Owls and a Hen,
    Five Larks and a Wren,
Have all built their nests in my Beard.'

Edward Lear

There was an Old Man who said: 'Hush!
I perceive a young bird in this bush!'
    When they asked: 'Is it small?'
    He replied: 'Not at all!
It is four times as big as the bush!'

Edward Lear

There was a Young Lady of Clare,
Who was sadly pursued by a bear;
　　When she found she was tired,
　　She abruptly expired,
That unfortunate Lady of Clare.

Edward Lear

There was a Young Lady whose folly
Induced her to sit on a holly;
　　Whereupon, by a thorn,
　　Her dress became torn.
She quickly became melancholy.

Edward Lear

There was an Old Man of Aosta,
Who possessed a large cow, but he lost her;
　　But they said: 'Don't you see
　　She has rushed up a tree?
You invidious Old Man of Aosta!'

Edward Lear

There was a young lady of Beccles,
Whose face was all covered in freckles;
　　　If it wasn't her face,
　　　It was some other place –
Perhaps it was Bungay, not Beccles?

G. B. Scott

There was an old woman from Keele,
Who longed to be friends with an eel;
　　　So she wove him a veil
　　　From his head to his tail –
That affectionate woman of Keele.

Ruth Silcock

Asked a Paris-bound traveller at Crewe:
'Does this fast express train go right through?'
　　　'There will be,' said the guard,
　　　As he looked at him hard,
'A most terrible splash if we do.'

T. L. McCarthy

There was an Old Man who, when little,
Fell casually into a Kettle;
　　　But, growing too stout,
　　　He could never get out,
And passed all his life in that Kettle.

Edward Lear

There was a young lady called Ida,
Whose mouth grew wider and wider;
    One dark winter's night,
    A man with poor sight
Dropped several postcards inside her.

Ron Rubin

There was an old person of Harrow,
Who bought a mahogany barrow;
    For he said to his wife:
    'You're the joy of my life,
And I'll wheel you all day in this barrow.'

Edward Lear

There was an old fellow of Tyre,
Who constantly sat on the fire;
    When asked: 'Is it hot?'
    He replied: 'No, it's not!
I'm James Winterbottom, Esquire.'

Anon.

A certain old person of Nigg,
Displayed a most far-reaching wig;
    When they said: 'You're too small!'
    He replied: 'Not at all!
It's the wig, I suspect, that's too big.'

N. M. Bodecker

Said a mournful old man of Larkhill:
'Each morning I take a green pill.
    It gives me bronchitis,
    The gout and gastritis,
But without it, I'm sure I'd feel ill.'

Frank Richards

Odd Bodikins

Such very odd bodies there be,
The strangest upon land or sea.
Such feet and such faces,
And things in odd places —
I'm thankful that none of them's me!

An old man who sat on the front
Did nothing but gurgle and grunt;
　　But those not at hand,
　　Thought it came from the band,
And encored this original stunt!

Anon.

A flatulent waiter named Welch
Loosed a world-record-breaking long belch;
　　It burped off at two,
　　Gurkled on all night through,
And ended at lunch with a squelch.

W. F. N. Watson

There was a young man of Devizes,
Whose ears were of different sizes;
　　The one that was small
　　Was no use at all,
But the other won several prizes.

Archibald Marshall

A tearful young person of Deeping
One night said: 'I must stop this weeping,
    Or else, I suppose,
    Learn to hang by my toes,
So as not to be drowned while I'm sleeping.'

N. M. Bodecker

Said a mixed-up young fellow named Pete:
'I can't tell my hands from my feet.
    It's fine round the town,
    When I walk upside down,
But I *do* bite my toes when I eat.'

Frank Richards

There was a young lady from Ware,
Who had an incredible stare.
    Her eyes were so good,
    She saw straight through wood,
And places you just wouldn't dare!

Robert Gray

There was a young lady of Flint
Who had a most horrible squint;
    She could scan the whole sky
    With her uppermost eye
While the other was reading small print.

Anon.

A singular fellow of Weston
Has near fifty feet of intestine;
    Though a signal success
    In the medical press,
It's not very good for digestin'.

Anon.

There was a young lady called Rose,
Who fainted whenever she chose;
    She did so one day,
    While playing croquet,
But was quickly revived with a hose.

Edward Gorey

There was a young fellow called Green,
Who grew so abnormally lean
    And flat and compressed,
    That his back met his chest,
And sideways he couldn't be seen.

Anon.

There was a young fellow called Pete
Who had the most delicate feet;
　　His feet were so lean,
　　He was told by the Queen:
'We have never seen feet quite so neat.'

Bland Tomkinson

A very strange fellow called Ned
Had eyes in the back of his head;
　　'There's no way of knowing
　　Which way I am going,
But I know where I've been to,' he said.

Frank Richards

There was a young woman of Thrace,
Whose nose spread all over her face.
　　She had very few kisses;
　　The reason for this is
There wasn't a suitable place.

Anon.

There was a young lady whose nose
Continually prospers and grows;
    When it grew out of sight,
    She exclaimed, in great fright:
'Oh! Farewell to the end of my nose!'

Edward Lear

    There was a young fellow of Kent,
    Whose nose was terribly bent;
        One day, I suppose,
        He could follow his nose,
    And no one would know where he went.

R. S. Saxby

    There was an old man of the Nore,
    The same shape behind as before;
        They didn't know where
        To offer a chair,
    So he had to sit down on the floor.

Anon.

It's not much fun being a toe,
What with bunions and nails that in-grow;
   And corns that get rubbed,
    Trodden on, nipped and stubbed,
And you can't even choose where you go.
                    Cyril Mountjoy

There was an old lady of Widnes
Well-renowned for her oversized kidneys;
   Should you mention their size
   She'd exclaim with surprise:
'They're not nearly as big as our Sidney's.'
              George McWilliam

Simply Fantastic!

Though it's simply fantastic! — don't boas
That you've seen a witch or a ghost.
If green men appear,
Is a UFO here,
Or was it too much cheese-on-toast?

As the audience whistled and jeered,
'I'll fix 'em,' the conjuror sneered.
  'Though they may be thick,
  I'll perform one more trick.'
He did, and they all disappeared.

Frank Richards

The people of Candlewood Knowles
Are terribly troubled by trolls,
  Who are driving their cars,
  And brawling in bars,
And voting for Thor at the polls.

Morris Bishop

A sea-serpent saw a big tanker,
Bit a hole in her side and then sank her;
  He swallowed the crew
  In a minute or two,
And then picked his teeth with the anchor.

Anon.

A man in the Bible once swore
A Martian had come to his door;
    He went to the sink
    Where he had a drink,
Then widdled all over the floor.

Spike Milligan

Said an Ogre from old Saratoga:
'I've tried to de-Ogre by Yoga;
    I've stood on my head
    All day in my bed,
But the mirror says I'm still an Ogre.'

Conrad Aiken

A Dragon who lives down at Staines,
Breathes flame at all low-flying planes;
    He roars: 'You'll catch fire,
    Unless you fly higher,
As witness this pile of remains!'

E. O. Parrott

The fabulous Wizard of Oz
Retired from business because
    What with up-to-date science,
    To most of his clients,
He wasn't the Wizard he woz.

Anon.

There was a young ghost named Paul,
Who went to a fancy dress ball;
    To shock every guest,
    He went there undressed,
But no one could see him at all.

Anon.

'Will you beam me up, Scotty? There's two
Space invaders preparing a stew.
    They have tied me up tightly,
    And salted me lightly . . .
Hey, Scotty! Am I getting through?'

T. L. McCarthy

There once was a wonderful wizard
Who got a fierce pain in his gizzard;
    So he drank wind and snow,
    At fifty below,
And farted a forty-mile blizzard.

Conrad Aiken

A wicked old witch of the west
Had curses tattooed on her chest,
    Which would turn into stone
    All that crossed the old crone,
But they burnt a great hole in her vest.

A. P. Cox

An astronaut, one afternoon,
Signalled: 'I'm coming down soon.
    I've had such a fright
    From a very strange sight —
A cow jumping over the moon!'

Frank Richards

When played by the phantoms of Shrule
Midnight football is eerie and cruel;
    If one kicks a ghost
    Past the other's goal-post,
He wins credit for scoring a ghoul.

Tony Butler

Moaned a ghost in a pub at Tralee:
'Will you please show your ticket to me?'
    So I did, and it went
    Through the wall, quite content —
It was just an inn-spectre, you see!

Frank Richards

The vampires that bite necks in gangs,
Like a blood that is tasty and tangs;
    When they've guzzled enough
    Of the hot pulsing stuff,
They say to their teeth: 'Thank you, fangs!'
                                    Tim Hopkins

King Wenceslas heard someone shout:
'There's a boy with a snowball about!'
    It went straight in his ear;
    Since when, every year,
The Good King has always looked out.
                                    Frank Richards

Said the Pied Piper: 'What shall I do?
These kids are an ill-mannered crew!
    I'd go back to the rats,
    If one of the brats
Hadn't bunged up my pipe with some glue!'
                                    Frank Richards

A princess who lived near a bog
Met a prince in the form of a frog;
    Now she and the prince
    Are the parents of quints –
Four boys and a fine polliwog.
                                    Ogden Nash

Mother Hubbard said: 'Poor Doggy, see –
This cupboard's as bare as can be!'
    Sneered the Dog: 'What a shame!
    You silly old dame!
It's because I've a duplicate key!'

Frank Richards

'Watch that Knave!' said the good Queen of Hearts:
'And inform me just when the fun starts!
    There's a handful of soil,
    Some stale castor-oil,
And a pound of cement in those tarts.'

Frank Richards

The Maid in the Garden was svelte,
And was hanging out clothes, when she felt
    A great bird, with a tweak,
    Take her nose in its beak,
After which, the maid no longer smelt.

Joyce Johnson

Miss Muffet's mum grew suspicious,
And asked: 'Was your dinner nutritious?'
    She replied: 'Curds and whey?
    I left them today!
I ate a big spider – delicious!'

Frank Richards

That inept young person, Miss Muffet,
Had further bad luck with her tuffet;
    Some used-tuffet dealers
    Decided to steal hers,
So now she must hire one – or rough it!

Dean Walley

The prince pleaded: 'Snow White, be mine!'
She answered: 'Oh, yes – how divine!
    Life will be Heaven,
    Not cooking for seven,
And without fourteen socks on the line!'

Frank Richards

Aladdin said, with a sly grin:
'I hold that strong drink is a sin.
   Though I rarely indulge,
   I am forced to divulge
That I owe my success to a djinn!'

                Frank Richards

'Ah, Goldilocks,' said Father Bear:
'I've been looking for you everywhere.
   I want ten pence, my pet,
   For the porridge you ate,
And I've got a small bill for a chair.'

                Frank Richards

'So you say Cinderella's your name?'
Said the constable: 'Have you no shame?
   It's twelve twenty-two.
   You've four mice and one shoe,
And a pumpkin in tow – what's your game?'

                Frank Richards

Silly People

Silly folk don't worry me –
I'm as silly as they are, you see;
I spread biscuits with glue,
Comb my hair with a shoe,
And eat kippers with custard for tea!

There was a young bard of Japan,
Whose limericks never would scan;
　　When told it was so,
　　He said: 'Yes, I know,
But I always try and get as many words
　　into the last line as I possibly can.'

Anon.

There was an old man of Blackheath,
Who sat down on his set of false teeth;
    Said he, with a start:
    'O Lord, bless my heart!
I have bitten myself underneath!'

                            Anon.

A Scotsman with very good sight,
Found a packet of corn-pads one night:
    'I won't waste them,' he thought;
    So the next day he bought
Some shoes that he knew were too tight.

                         Ida Thurtle

A furious man in a tree
Said: 'What's all this Nature to me?
    I've looked at the view –
    Now what do I do?
I ought to have brung my TV.'

                       N. M. Bodecker

There was an old farmer of Watton,
Who planted his fields full of cotton;
    When nothing would grow,
    He wanted to know
If the reels he had planted were rotten.

C. K. Thompson

Said a foolish young oarsman called Clout:
'This bath's a fine boat, there's no doubt.
    I'm sure I shall win,
    And if water gets in,
There's a plug-hole to let it run out.'

E. O. Parrott

There was a young man, name of Fred,
Who spent every Thursday in bed;
    He lay with his feet
    Outside of the sheet,
And the pillows on top of his head.

Edward Gorey

A tiresome old person of Corning,
Just wouldn't get up in the morning;
    When they said: 'Tell us why!'
    She made some reply,
Though they couldn't hear what for her yawning.

                          N. M. Bodecker

    A playful young lady of York,
    Accidentally swallowed a cork;
        But she didn't complain,
        Though it gave her some pain,
    She just pushed it down with a fork.

                        Robert McBean Tidey

There was an old person of Duns,
Who said: 'I'll eat ninety-three buns.'
    At the seventy-first,
    He unhappily burst,
So the rest were consumed by his sons.

                        Langford Reed

Said a mountaineer in a Swiss town:
'I'm an expert who's won great renown.
    I've climbed every one,
    But my new way's more fun:
I start at the top – and climb down.'

Frank Richards

Said a boastful young student from Hayes,
As he entered the Hampton Court maze:
    'There's nothing in it!
    I won't be a minute.'
He's been missing for forty-three days.

Frank Richards

There was a young seedsman of Leeds,
Who once swallowed a packet of seeds;
    In a month – silly ass! –
    He was covered in grass,
And he couldn't sit down for the weeds.

Anon.

A respectable lady of Troon
Became very strange at full moon;
    She danced on the rose-bed
    Until her poor toes bled,
And sang: 'I'm a prune! I'm a prune!'

Wendy Cope

Said a convict in prison in Sale:
'My tunnel's superb! It can't fail!'
    Through April and May,
    He dug night and day,
Then came up inside Brixton Gaol!

Frank Richards

At a café, the man next to me
Ordered twenty-two candles for tea;
    When I murmured: 'How quaint!'
    He replied: 'No, I ain't.
I'm on a light diet, you see.'

Frank Richards

There was a young fellow called Willy,
Who acted remarkably silly;
    At an All-Nations ball,
    Dressed in nothing at all,
He claimed that his costume was Chile.

Anon.

There was a young sailor called Pink,
Whose mates rushed him off to the clink;
    He said: 'I've a skunk
    As a pet in my bunk –
That's no reason for raising a stink.'

                            Anon.

There was a young man of Cawnpore,
Whom people mistook for a door;
    When the postman came by,
    He would heave a great sigh:
'Eating letters,' he said, 'is a bore.'

                        Ruth Silcock

There was a young man from Darjeeling,
Who boarded a bus bound for Ealing;
    He saw on the door:
    'Please don't spit on the floor.'
So he carefully spat on the ceiling.

                            Anon.

A rather vague person of Rame,
Just could not remember her name;
    When someone from Scones
    Said: 'My name is Jones.'
She said: 'Oh, perhaps mine's the same.'

                    N. M. Bodecker

A silly young man of Thames Ditton
Has climbed every church spire in Britain;
 He says: 'What I like
 Is each has a spike,
Which makes it so comfy to sit on.'

       E. O. Parrott

The funniest man that I've met
Keeps a very large rock as a pet;
 It's as quiet as a mouse,
 Makes no mess in the house,
And he never pays bills to the vet.

       Frank Richards

A pianist named Clyde once cried:
'This piano stays locked, though I've tried.'
 His wife said: 'You goose!
 It's really no use!
Don't you know that the keys are inside?'

      Harriet Mandelbaum

A clever young farmer named Binns
Fed his cows on scrap metal and pins;
    It was always the same –
    When milking-time came,
It was neatly delivered in tins.

                             Frank Richards

Young Jimmy would not go to bed,
But stayed watching telly instead;
    As he stayed up to stare,
    His face went all square,
And an aerial grew out of his head.

                             Frank Richards

Screamed a nervous young fellow from Kelling:
'On my face there's a terrible swelling!'
    His doctor said: 'Rot!
    You silly young clot!
It's only your nose – stop your yelling!'

                             Frank Richards

Sad Ends

The limerick's now forced to tell
Of sad ends that to some folk befell;
May the lessons be learned,
The moral not spurned,
Or I might write of your end, as well.

Snapping animals near the equator,
A camera-mad game-park spectator
        Said: 'It's easy, you see!
        So, someone take me!'
And was snapped — by a huge alligator.

                              Gerry Hamill

A careless explorer called Blake,
Fell into a tropical lake;
    Said a fat alligator,
    A few minutes later:
'Very nice, but I still prefer cake.'

Ogden Nash

There was a young lady of Ryde,
Who was carried too far by the tide;
    A man-eating shark
    Said: 'How's this for a lark?
I knew that the Lord would provide.'

Anon.

There was a young fellow called Clyde,
Who once at a funeral was spied;
    When asked who was dead,
    He smilingly said:
'I don't know – I just came for the ride.'

Anon.

There was an old Sultan of Jeddah,
Who loved English cheeses like Cheddar;
    One day he quite fancied
    A piece that was rancid,
And now there is nobody deader.

Ron Rubin

There once was an eccentric old boffin,
Who remarked, in a fine fit of coughin':
    'It isn't the cough
    That carries you off,
But the coffin they carry you off in.'

Anon.

There was a young lady called Plunnery,
Who rejoiced in the practice of gunnery;
    One day, unobservant,
    She blew up a servant,
And had to retire to a nunnery.

Edward Gorey

There was a young man of the Tyne,
Put his head on the South-Eastern line;
　　But he died of *ennui*,
　　For the 5.53
Didn't run till a quarter past nine.

　　　　　　　　　　　　　　Anon.

Said a gleeful young man of Tor Bay:
'This is rather a red-letter day,
　　For I've poisoned the sherbet
　　Of rich Uncle Herbert,
Whose health *never* seemed to decay!'

　　　　　　　　　　　　　　Anon.

A careless old cook of Saltash
In her second-hand car had a crash;
　　She drove through a wall,
　　House, garden and all,
And ended up Banger-and-Mash.

　　　　　　　　　　　　　　Anon.

A boastful young fellow of Neath,
Once hung from the roof by his teeth;
　　A very large crowd
　　First cheered him quite loud,
Then passed round the hat for a wreath.

　　　　　　　　　　　　Frank Richards

There was a young lady of Gloucester,
Whose mother and father once lost her;
    Next day she was found
    On the icy-cold ground,
And they couldn't find how to defrost her.

Thomas McDonald

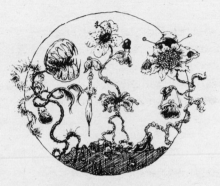

There was a young lady of Nantes,
Who was troubled by certain old aunts;
    So she buried the lot
    In her vegetable plot,
And grew some remarkable plants.

Colin Shaw

A ticket-collector named Fred,
Punched tickets expertly, they said;
    But alas and alack!
    One punched him right back,
So he dropped them all quickly, and fled.

Vincent Mulholland

A short-sighted housewife called Jean
Read: 'A Quick Way to Melt Gelatine'.
    She applied a fierce light
    To some raw gelignite –
Since that moment she hasn't been seen.

Frank Richards

There was an old man in a hearse,
Who murmured: 'This might have been worse.
    Of course, the expense
    Is simply immense,
But it doesn't come out of my purse.'

Anon.

There was a young fellow called Hyde,
Who fell down a privy and died;
    His unfortunate brother
    Fell into another,
And now they're interred side by side.

Anon.

Said a foolish young housewife of Wales:
'A smell of escaped gas prevails.'
    So she searched with a light,
    And, later that night,
Was collected in several pails.

Langford Reed

An intrepid explorer called Bliss
Fell into a gorge or abyss,
    But remarked as he fell:
    'Oh, I might just as well
Get right to the bottom of this.'

N. M. Bodecker

The babe, with a cry brief and dismal,
Fell into the waters baptismal;
    Ere they gathered its plight,
    It had sunk out of sight,
For the depths of that font were abysmal.

Edward Gorey

A serious young lady from Welwyn,
Took a cookery book to Helvellyn;
    While reading the recipes,
    She fell over a precipice,
And that was the end of poor Ellen.

C. Armstrong Gibbs

There was a young man from the city,
Who met what he thought was a kitty;
    He gave it a pat,
    And said: 'Nice little cat!'
They buried his clothes out of pity.

Anon.

A jolly young fellow of Yuma,
Told an elephant joke to a puma;
    Now his skeleton lies
    Beneath hot western skies –
For that puma had no sense of huma.

Ogden Nash

There was a young lady of Looe,
Caught a terrible dose of the 'flu;
    She wheezed till a cough
    Caused her head to drop off –
So mind it don't happen to you!

Michelle Games

The Hoover in grim silence sat,
But sucking no more at the mat;
    Quietly it grunted,
    As slowly it shunted,
And messily disgorged the cat.

David Woodsford

There was a young lady called Harris,
Whom nothing seemed apt to embarrass,
    Till the bath-salts she shook
    In the bath that she took,
Turned out to be plaster of Paris.

Ogden Nash

An artist who lives in St Ives,
Collected quaint African knives,
    But his children all thought
    They were there for their sport —
Out of eight, only one now survives.

A. G. Prys-Jones

Not Wholly Holy

We move to the vicarage now,
And a Bishop or two make their bow;
*   There's more than one joke*
*   About such reverend folk,*
For a few aren't as holy as thou.

There was a young lady of Tottenham,
Her manners, she'd wholly forgotten 'em;
    While at tea at the Vicar's,
    She took off her knickers,
Explaining she felt much too hot in 'em.

Anon.

The robes of the Vicar of Cheltenham
Gave pleasure whenever he knelt in 'em,
    But they got rather hot
    When he wore them a lot,
And the Vicar of Cheltenham smelt in 'em.

Anon.

A Brother, when asked by the Prior,
Why he spent so much time by the fire,
    Said: 'While all of you pray,
    I sit here all day —
In fact, I'm your chip-monk, or friar.'

Anon.

A miserly Bishop of Norwich
Told his choirboys: 'For food, you must forwich!'
    They went gleaning for oats,
    Like a herd of wild goats —
Then filled up his mitre with porwich.

A. P. Cox

There was a young girl in the choir,
Whose voice rose higher and higher,
    Till one Sunday night,
    It rose quite out of sight,
And they found it next day on the spire.

Anon.

We thought him an absolute lamb,
Until he sat down on the jam,
    On taking his seat
    At the Sunday School treat –
We all heard our Vicar say: 'Stand up, please while
    I say grace.'

Anon.

There was a young fellow of Ceuta,
Who rode into church on his scooter;
    He knocked down the Dean,
    And said: 'Sorry, old bean!
I ought to have sounded my hooter.'

Anon.

There once was a pious young priest,
Who lived almost wholly on yeast;
    'For,' he said, 'it is plain
    We must all rise again,
And I want to get started, at least.'

Langford Reed

A clergyman, out in Dumont,
Keeps tropical fish in his font;
    Though it always surprises
    The babes he baptises,
It seems to be just what they want.

Morris Bishop

There were three young women of Birmingham,
And I know a sad story concerning 'em:
    They stuck needles and pins
    In the Right Reverend shins
Of the Bishop engaged in confirming 'em.

Anon.

There were three little owls in a wood,
Who sang hymns whenever they could;
    What the words were about
    One could never make out,
But one felt it was doing them good.

Anon.

There was an old person of Fratton,
Who would go to church with his hat on;
    'When I wake up,' he said,
    'With my hat on my head,
I shall know that it hasn't been sat on.'

Anon.

Archbishops

Archbishops are terribly rare.
They don't just crop up anywhere.
    If you meet face to face
    You should murmur: 'Your Grace!'
Most politely, and try not to stare.

Mary Holtby

Bishops

They have surnames like Cicestr: or Oxon:
In church they put smart party frocks on;
    In fact they're so grand
    That there's none in the land
Who has witnessed them putting their socks on.

Mary Holtby

There was an old Bishop of Salisbury,
Who said: 'Trousers? I simply can't balisbury!'
    Said the Archbishop (Canterbury):
    'What a great elephanterbury!
You're too halisbury-scalisbury to walisbury!'

Paul Griffin

Curious Tales

Some stories are so odd and curious,
That they probably are mostly spurious.
But if they were true
And happened to you,
I suspect that you'd be really furious.

There was an old man in the queue,
Who talked for an hour of the 'flu;
    So infectious his tale,
    He himself grew quite pale –
Now the rest of the queue has the 'flu.

                               W. Stewart

A conjuror hailing from Hunts.,
Who did most spectacular stunts,
    Took too many risks
    When juggling with discs,
Thus breaking five records at once.

Joyce Johnson

There was a young lady of Ealing,
Who walked up and down on the ceiling;
    She shouted: 'Oh, heck!
    I have broken my neck,
And it is a most curious feeling.'

Anon.

There was a young man of Bengal,
Who went to a fancy-dress ball;
    He went as a tree,
    But failed to foresee
What was done by the dog in the hall.

Anon.

A two-toothed old man of Arbroath
Gave vent to a terrible oath;
When one tooth chanced to ache,
By an awful mistake,
The dentist extracted them both.

Anon.

I know a young fellow from Leek,
Who, instead of a nose, has a beak;
Every day – it's absurd –
He grows more like a bird
(He migrates at the end of next week).

Frank Richards

A thrifty soprano of Hingham,
Designed her own dresses of gingham;
On the blue and white squares,
She wrote opera airs,
So when they wore out, she could singham.

Ogden Nash

A cannibal friend, I regret,
Has gone down with a stomach upset;
     The doctor said: 'Bill,
     I can guess why you're ill.
It must have been someone you ate!'

Ron Rubin

An eccentric old man of Mill Hill
Decided to make a new will;
     He left all the 'loot'
     To Elaine, his pet newt,
On condition she moved to Brazil.

Wendy Cope

An old Indian chief, Running B'ar,
At making it rain was a star:
     When asked: 'How do you do it?'
     He replied: 'Nothing to it!
To make rain, me just washum car.'

Mary Rita Hurley

There was an old hag of Malacca,
Who smoked *such* atrocious tobacca,
     When tigers came near,
     They trembled with fear,
And did not attempt to attaca.

Anon.

A Red Indian said: 'I have spoken!
Of my friendship I'll give you a token.
    The time is now ripe
    To smoke piece of pipe,
Because pipe of peace has got broken.'

Frank Richards

A strong-minded lady of Arden
Grows nothing but burrs in her garden;
    She tosses the burrs
    On passing chauffeurs,
And never begs anyone's pardon.

Morris Bishop

An architect sat back and laughed:
'I know that my new plans seem daft.
    On each of the floors,
    There's no windows or doors –
But at least I've got rid of the draught.'

Frank Richards

68

There was an old man of Peru,
Who dreamt he was eating his shoe;
    He awoke in the night
    With a terrible fright,
And found it was perfectly true.

Anon.

There was a young lady of Twickenham
Whose boots were too tight to walk quickenham;
    She bore them awhile,
    But at last, at a stile,
She pulled them both off and was sickenham.

Anon.

There once was a person of Benin,
Who wore clothes not fit to be seen in;
    When told that he shouldn't,
    He replied: 'Gumscrumrudent!'
A word of inscrutable meanin'.

Anon.

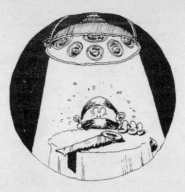

A competitive surgeon from Boulder
Once removed his own arm at the shoulder,
    Then did a repeat,
    With one hand, on both feet,
The record stands, but not the holder.

J. Michie

There was a young farmer called Max,
Who avoided petroleum tax;
    It was simple, you see,
    For his Vespa burned pee
From his grandfather's herd of tame yaks.

Anon.

A bugler named Douglas McDougal
Found ingenious ways to be frugal;
    He learned how to sneeze
    In various keys,
Thus saving the price of a bugle.

Ogden Nash

There was a young lady of Spain,
Who couldn't go out in the rain,
      For she'd lent her umbrella
      To Queen Isabella,
Who never returned it again.

Anon.

An Australian native one day
Bought a new boomerang with his pay,
      But he broke down and cried,
      For, however he tried,
He could not throw the old one away.

Frank Richards

Said a micro-chip-maker from Slough:
'My latest invention's a wow!
      I have indexed and stored,
      On a one-inch-square board,
The whole of creation till now!'

Michael Lee

A daring young stunt-man named Jack
Dived three hundred feet in a sack,
      But when half-way down,
      He feared he would drown –
So he just changed his mind, and went back.

Frank Richards

There was a young fellow of Perth,
Who was born on the day of his birth;
    He was married, they say,
    On his wife's wedding day,
And he died when he quitted this earth.

Anon.

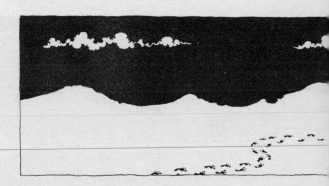

There was a young man of Kuwait,
Who went out one night for a date;
    He climbed up a palm,
    With hardly a qualm,
And there found his date, which he ate.

Ron Rubin

The Britons of old had a mode
Of wearing smart costumes of woad –
    A kind of blue paint.
    They must have looked quaint –
And I bet they were cold when it snowed!

Langford Reed

An Arab, whose name was Omar,
Kept a camel instead of a car;
    He filled up at oases,
    And other such places.
(More miles to the gallon, by far!)

Frank Richards

There was a young lady of Spain,
Who was terribly sick in a train,
    Not once, but again,
    And again and again,
And again, and again . . . AND AGAIN.

Anon.

There was a young person called Briggs,
Whose hair grew like branches and twigs;
    When she watered her toes
    With a small garden hose,
It produced the most wonderful figs.

N. M. Bodecker

Home Affairs

No matter how far you may roam,
It's agreed that there's no place like home,
    Or so runs the song –
    But things can go wrong,
And give rise to a limerick pome.

Said the mother of Daniel Chalk:
'Your new little sister can't talk,
    But screams loudly, I fear.'
    Said Dan: 'Mother, dear,
I'd much rather we'd kept the stork.'

E. O. Parrott

There was a young girl of Asturias,
Whose temper was frantic and furious;
    She used to throw eggs
    At her grandmother's legs,
A habit unpleasant, though curious.

Anon.

There was an old couple of Ryde,
Who walked out for years, side by side;
    He said: 'Years have we tarried —
    It's time we were married.'
'You fool, who would have us?' she cried.

George McWilliam

There's nothing so potent as mumps,
For putting you down in the dumps;
    You feel frumpy and grumpy
    And jumpy and humpy,
Because of those terrible lumps.

D. C. Barker

My Dad, who's as bald as a bat,
Spilt hair tonic over the mat;
    Now it's grown so much higher,
    We can't see the fire,
And we've searched it in vain for the cat.

Frank Richards

A scatter-brained couple from Gissing,
Arranged for an afternoon christening;
    When they got there, she said:
    'Where's the baby then, Ted?'
He replied: 'I *thought* something was missing.'

Ida Thurtle

Elizabeth Boggart of Dene,
Once fell in the washing-machine;
    Her mother said: 'Lizzie,
    Although you feel dizzy,
It's the first time you've ever been clean.'

Frank Richards

There was an old farmer of Slough
Who harnessed a mule to his plough;
    Should you ask him why
    He was apt to reply:
'Well, my wife is too old for this now!'
George McWilliam

There was an old fellow of Gosham,
Who took out his false teeth to wash 'em;
    His wife said: 'Oh, Jack!
    If you don't put them back,
I'll jump on the dam' things and squash 'em.'
Anon.

A youngster from near Bodmin Moor
Found bathing a terrible chore;
    He muttered: 'Oh, heck!
    This shirt covers my neck,
So why need I wash any more?'
Betty Morris

I have watched my pet rabbits at play,
And looked at my mice twice a day;
    I *know* – I'm not dumb –
    Where babies come from,
But why doesn't anyone say?
Anon.

A maggot decided to stop
With a girl-friend he met in a shop;
    They married in haste
    In a mound of meat paste,
But now they've moved into a chop.

                         Cyril Mountjoy

A handyman once made a boast:
'Repairing is what I like most.'
    Now his cooker can play
    Lively music all day,
While the radio burns all the toast.

                         Frank Richards

There was a young rascal from Hastings,
Who suffered some well-deserved bastings,
    And was smacked even harder
    When found in the larder,
Enjoying unauthorized tastings.

                         Langford Reed

Dad waited while Mum bought the ham,
But when she came out, she said: 'Sam!
    That one's not our baby!'
    He answered: 'Well, maybe,
But look, it's a much better pram!'

Coral Copping

There was a young fellow named Hammer,
Who had an unfortunate stammer;
    'The bane of my life,'
    Said he, 'is my wife!
D . . . d . . . d . . . d . . . d . . . d . . . damn her!'

Anon.

I once thought a lot of a friend,
Who turned out to be, in the end,
    The most southerly part
    (As I'd feared from the start)
Of a horse with a northerly trend.

Anon.

There once was a baby of yore,
Whose parents found it a bore,
    And being afraid
    That it might get mislaid,
They stored it away in a drawer.

Anon.

Eat, Drink . . . and Be Merry?

These limericks talk about food,
Dishes simmered and sautéed and stewed;
Concoctions delicious,
Occasions auspicious,
And manners, both seemly and rude.

An eccentric old person of Slough,
Who took all his meals with a cow,
    Always said: 'It's uncanny,
    She's so like Aunt Fanny!'
But he never would indicate how.

George Robey

Overeating was Susie's disgrace;
She'd an appetite vulgar and base,
    And the food that she gobbled
    Soon afterwards wobbled
At the opposite end from her face.

Tim Hopkins

I went with the Duchess to tea;
Her manners were shocking to see;
    Her rumblings abdominal,
    Were simply phenomenal,
And everyone thought it was me!

Woodrow Wilson

A trader named Sandy McVeetie,
With a cannibal chief made a treaty;
    In a glass of gin-sling,
    Mac toasted the king,
And then the king . . . toasted McVeetie.

F. J. Smith

Said a gentleman dining in Papua
To his friend: 'What an awfully good chap you are!
　　To allow me to share
　　Your delicious *grandmère*,
But you're dropping her bones in my lap, you are!'

Ron Rubin

There once was a cannibal called Ned
Who used to eat onions in bed;
　　His Mother said: 'Sonny,
　　It's not very funny –
Why don't you eat people instead?'

Anon.

A missionary lady named Price
Said: 'The Chinese are not very nice.
　　When I asked if they knew
　　What there was in the stew,
They bowed with a smile and said: "Lice!"'

B. Ridley

'What makes you think I'm feeling sick,
After only five pancakes?' asked Dick.
    'Six iced buns, some chops,
    And four ginger pops?
I'm fine . . . Where's the bathroom? . . . And quick!'
Frank Richards

There was a young lady called Perkins,
Exceedingly fond of small gherkins;
    She went out to tea,
    And ate forty-three,
Which pickled her internal werkins.

Anon.

A glutton who lived on the Rhine,
Was asked at what hour he would dine;
    He replied: 'At eleven,
    At three, five, and seven,
At eight, and a quarter past nine.'

Anon.

There was a young man of St Just,
Who ate apple-pie till he bust;
    It wasn't the fru-it
    That caused him to do it —
What finished him off was the crust!

Anon.

A strange fellow once said to me:
'I'm hungry for music, you see.'
    He devoured a drum,
    And a euphonium,
And ate a piano-for-te.

Frank Richards

There's a whimsical fellow in Deal,
Who barks for his food, like a seal;
    Says his wife, with a sniff:
    'It would be funnier if
He'd skip an occasional meal.'

Morris Bishop

In her den 'neath an African sky,
Said a leopardess, heaving a sigh,
    To her hungry young leopards:
    'We've run out of shepherds!
Tonight there'll be no shepherd's pie!'

T. L. McCarthy

There once was an ancient Peruvian,
Whose manners were antediluvian;
    After bolting his food,
    He was often so rude
As to belch in a manner Vesuvian.

Richard Kent Heller

There once was a person of Bude,
Who was such an incredible prude,
    That she got in a state o-
    ver peeling potato
And serving it up in the nude.

Anon.

An epicure, dining at Crewe,
Found a rather large mouse in his stew;
    Said the waiter: 'Don't shout,
    And wave it about,
Or the rest will be wanting one too.'

Anon.

A young girl who was fond of meringue,
Let thoughts of her figure go hingue;
    She ate them in tons,
    Along with cream buns,
Until she went off with a bingue.

Val Pöhler

There once was a cook of Loch Ness,
Whose dishes were not a success;
    She once had a bash
    At bangers and mash –
And you never yet sausage a mess!

Ron Rubin

There was a young fellow named Sam,
Who loved tucking into the jam;
    When his mother said: 'Sammy,
    Don't make yourself jammy!',
He said: 'You're too late, Ma. I am!'

Langford Reed

There was a young lady called Mears,
Whose remarks brought her parents to tears:
    'Now melon is nice,
    But the shape of the slice
Causes moisture to drip from the ears.'

Robert McBean Tidey

All Creatures Great and Small

The limerick now will recall
All creatures that live, great or small;
*   Bird, fish, or mammal,*
*   From the bee to the camel —*
And throw some new light on them all.

There was a young girl of Madras,
Who had a magnificent ass;
 It was not round and pink,
 As you possibly think –
It was grey, had long ears, and ate grass.

Anon.

There was a small dog of Pirbright,
Who would play on the organ all night;
 And in this shrewd way,
 Kept the burglars away,
For its Bach was far worse than its bite.

R. MacDonald

There was a small maiden called Maggie,
Whose dog was enormous and shaggy;
 The face end of him
 Looked fierce and grim,
But the tail end was friendly and waggy.

Langford Reed

A French poodle espied in the hall
A pool a damp gamp had let fall,
    And said: '*Ah, oui, oui!*
    This time it's not me,
But I'm bound to be blamed for it all.'

Anon.

An animal breeder from Leigh
Had a dog that was strange as could be;
    When told: 'But your hound
    Makes a loud ticking sound!'
He explained: 'It's a watch-dog, you see.'

Frank Richards

Of a sudden the great prima donna
Cried: 'Gaawd! My voice is a gonner!'
    But a cat, in the wings
    Said: 'I know how she sings.'
And finished the solo with honour.

Anon.

A rooster of greatest renown
Fought a duck in a neighbouring town,
    And when he had licked her,
    'Give up!' crowed the victor;
'I can't,' quacked the duck, 'I give down!'

Harriet Mandelbaum

There was an old woman of Clackmore,
Who threw out a flat-iron by the back-door;
    By a bit of bad luck,
    It fell on a duck,
And that duck was ne'er known to quack more.
Traditional Buckinghamshire Rhyme

Forgive me now, please, if I burble –
It's all on account of my djerbil,
    Who ran off today,
    With a hamster called Mae –
It's no wonder I'm feeling so terbil.
Alan Clark

There once were two cats of Kilkenny;
Each thought there was one cat too many,
    So they quarrelled and fit,
    They scratched and they bit,
    Till, barring their nails,
    And the tips of their tails,
Instead of two cats, there weren't any.
Anon.

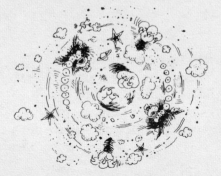

A considerate cow – it was brown –
Saw the milkmaid was looking run-down;
  'Don't worry, my dear,'
  The cow said: 'Sit here,
And hang on, while I jump up and down.'
         Paul Alexander

Said an old Sussex sow: 'Though I curse,
Things might have been very much worse.
  If my ears had been such
  They were silky to touch,
Each might have been took for a purse.'
         E. O. Parrott

There was a young person of Berks,
So exceedingly partial to sharks,
  That she kept a small school
  Of these fish in a pool,
And taught them to make rude remarks.
         Hic

From Ceylon to the island of Sark,
A fish to be feared is the shark;
  With its horrible whim
  For a raw human limb,
Its bite is far worse than its bark.
         Willy Tadpole

'He's a queer-looking cove is the flounder,'
Said the cod to the hake, 'and a bounder.
      The whisper is rife
      That he murdered his wife –
The flounder, the bounder, just drowned her.'

Cleoulston

How often and often I wish
I lived in green depths like a fish!
      No noise. Not a thing,
      Save the mermaids who sing,
Whilst their tails give a silvery swish.

Frances Cornford

A sensitive fish is the gudgeon,
Much given to umbrage and dudgeon;
      It cannot stand chaff,
      So please do not laugh
At its efforts to master the trudgeon.

Leslie Johnson

Said a winkle: 'I wish I was thin.
This shell is so cramped when I'm in.
      I'm so terribly stout
      That I'll never get out!
Can somebody lend me a pin?'

Frank Richards

A mathematician named Lynch
To a centipede said: 'It's a cinch!
    When your legs I've reckoned,
     I'll know in a second
Just how many feet in an inch!'

Harriet Mandelbaum

Said a puzzled young gardener named Sue,
Who had just cut a poor worm in two:
    'Oh, I know I'm to blame,
     But both ends look the same!
So which do I say "Sorry" to?'

E. O. Parrott

A wasp on a nettle said: 'Coo!
We're in a right mess, me and you.
    We have got to sort out
     What this is about.
Please tell me – who's got to sting who?'

Frank Richards

A rare old bird is the pelican;
His beak holds more than his belican.
    He can take in his beak
    Enough food for a week.
I'm darned if I know how the helican.

Dixon Merritt

A talented young chimpanzee
Was keen to appear on TV;
    So he wrote to Brooke Bond,
    Who did not respond,
So he had to become an M.P.

Wendy Cope

There was an old lady of Guise,
Who kept two performing tame fleas
    Named Cuthbert and Kate,
    Who did tricks on a plate,
And earned quite respectable fees.

Langford Reed

A handsome young rodent named Gratian
As a life-guard became a sensation;
    All the lady mice waved,
    And screamed to be saved
By his mouse-to-mouse resuscitation.

Ogden Nash

A monkey exclaimed with some glee:
'The things in this Zoo that I see!
    The comical features
    Of all those strange creatures
Who keep throwing peanuts at me!'

Frank Richards

A barber who lived in Batavia
Was well-known for his fearless behaviour;
    An enormous baboon
    Broke in his saloon,
But he murmured: 'I'm blowed if I'll shave yer!'

Anon.

A famous white hunter from Tottenham
Rose up one fine day from his ottoman,
    And shot seven llamas
    In his pink pyjamas –
'I wonder,' he mused, 'how they got in 'em?'

Ron Rubin

A monkey who lived in the zoo,
Was spoiling for something to do;
    A lady came in
    And tickled its chin –
What a pity that hat was brand new!

Robert McBean Tidey

A kangaroo baby named Fred
Said: 'Mother, it's time that I fled.
    There are too many ouches
    For babies in pouches,
When others eat biscuits in bed.'

Peter Alexander

An animal hunter was fined
For corrupting a young lady's mind;
    He'd said: 'Near the Cape –
    What a narrow escape! –
I ran miles with a great bear behind!'

Frank Richards

A cheerful old bear at the Zoo
Could always find something to do;
    When it bored him to go
    On a walk to and fro,
He reversed it, and walked fro and to.

Anon.

An elephant born in Tibet,
One day in his cage wouldn't get;
    So its keeper stood near,
    Stuck a hose in its ear,
And invented the first Jumbo Jet.

Anon.

A sheik from the mountains of Riff,
Returned from a journey, said: 'If
    Camels had wheels
    Like automobiles,
I would surely be feeling less stiff.'

N. M. Bodecker

If you wish to descend from a camel,
That oddly superior mammal,
    You just have to jump
    From that hump on its rump;
He won't just stop dead like a tram'll.

Anon.

Said a vet as he looked at my pet:
'That's the skinniest bear that I've met.
    I'll soon alter that.'
    Now the bear's nice and fat.
The question is — where is the vet?

Frank Richards

A tiger with tastes anthropophagous,
Felt a yearning within his oesophagus.
    He spied a fat Brahmin,
    And growled: 'What's the harm in
A peripatetic sarcophagus?'

Anon.

There was a young lady of Riga
Who smiled as she rode on a tiger;
    They returned from the ride
    With the lady inside,
And the smile on the face of the tiger.

Cosmo Monkhouse

A hyena once bet he could laugh
A lot louder than any giraffe;
    Hyenas, please note –
    A giraffe has a throat
That produces a laugh and a half.

Bill Greenwell

Said a young armadillo: 'It's sad,
But I can't snuggle up to my Dad,
    For an old armadillo
    Makes a very bad pillow,
Because of the way that he's clad.'

Peter Alexander

There once was a Plesiosaurus,
Who lived when the earth was all porous;
    But it fainted with shame
    When it first heard its name,
And departed long ages before us.

Anon.

An ostrich named Hullaballoo,
Said: 'Father, will I be like you,
    And be able to stand
      With my head in the sand,
So I'll be invisible too?'

Peter Alexander

School and Sport

All children need some kind of school,
Or each may turn out a fool;
*   And the practice of sport*
*   Gives you skill of a sort,*
And real fun as a general rule.

A pretty schoolmistress called Beauchamp
Said: 'These awful boys, how shall I teauchamp?
    For they will not behave,
    Although I look grave,
And with tears in my eyes, I beseauchamp!'
Langford Reed

A silly young schoolboy called Kipps
Sat in science class, smacking his lips;
    He said: 'I could wish
    For a silicon fish,
To go with these silicon chips.'
E. O. Parrott

A clumsy young schoolgirl called Bessie
Had to write on the Battle of Crécy;
    As she sat down to think,
    She knocked over the ink –
Bessie's essay on Crécy *was* messy!
Frank Richards

A Lollipop Lady from Poole
Felt one day like playing the fool,
    And that's what she did:
    She stopped every kid,
And sent fifteen lorries to school.
Frank Richards

A History master of Tottenham
Said: 'My dates, I have clearly forgotten 'em.
　　I knew them quite well,
　　But at present (Oh Hell!)
There is nothing else for it but swotten' 'em
George McWilliam

A girl from a nice convent school,
Was wicked, sadistic and cruel;
　　One night, just for fun,
　　She set fire to a nun,
Screaming: 'Oh, what a silly old fuel!'
Spike Milligan

A humourless teacher called Hills
Cured insomnia without using pills;
　　His words, dull and boring,
　　Led quickly to snoring,
For such were his medical skills.
Tim Hopkins

A silly school-leaver called Norman
Applied for a job as a doorman.
  When told they had three,
  Said Norman: 'I see!
Then maybe you'll make me the foreman.'

          E. O. Parrott

There was a young man from the Cam,
Who took an important exam;
  When he asked: 'Have I passed?'
  They replied: 'No, you're last.'
He turned on his heel and said: 'Gentlemen, you
 surprise me.'

            Anon.

There was a young schoolgirl of Rhyl,
Whose general knowledge was nil;
  She thought Joan of Arc
  Navigated the bark
That landed on Ararat's hill.

            Anon.

A prim little schoolgirl from Ford,
At getting good conduct marks scored;
  She'd no time for boys,
  Called pop music 'noise',
And was terribly, terribly bored.

          E. O. Parrott

Our teacher's a bit of a bore;
Still, I'll say this, when he takes the floor,
    You can have a short snooze,
    More or less when you choose,
But you're NEVER permitted to snore.

                      T. L. McCarthy

There was a young man of Belfast,
Who ran in a race and came last;
    He said: 'That's enough!
    I'm all out of puff,'
As a tortoise came thundering past.

                      Carl Stevenson

There was a young fellow called Tribbling,
Whose hobby was basket-ball dribbling,
    But he dribbled one day
    On a busy free-way —
Now his sisters are lacking a sibling.

                      Dean Walley

Said a runner who raced in Argyll,
As he tried for the two-minute mile:
      'I know I can win it
      In less than a minute –
I'll just hang around for a while.'

                                  E. O. Parrott

There was a young lady of Venice,
Who used hard-boiled eggs to play tennis.
      When they said: 'It is wrong.'
      She replied: 'Go along!
You don't know how prolific my hen is.'

                                  Anon.

Yelled a jockey at Epsom race-course,
As he galloped with hurricane force:
      'I've beaten the lot!'
      But the crowd cried: 'You clot!
Go back! You've forgotten your horse!'

                                  Frank Richards

A Yorkshire Limerick

There was a young lady from Hull,
Who had a fierce fight with a bull;
    It tossed her up twice –
    She said it was nice,
But perhaps just a little bit dull!

                          Susan Emanuel

Said a footballer once at Torquay:
'A chance for a goal now I see!'
    With a most skilful flick,
    He gave a great kick,
And levelled the score in Dundee.

                          Frank Richards

There was a young man from Crewe,
Who wanted to build a canoe;
    He went to the river
    And found, with a shiver,
He hadn't used waterproof glue.

                          Lorna Bain

A sporting young athlete from Fleet
Was a sprinter that no one could beat;
    So he fixed on a stunt,
    And ran back to front,
And won by a very short seat.

                          Frank Richards

There was an old man of Bengal,
Who purchased a bat and a ball,
    Some gloves and some pads –
    It was one of his fads,
For he never played cricket at all.

F. Anstey

A young angler landed a dace,
That had whiskers all over its face;
    Said a passer-by: 'That fish
    Is surely a cat-fish,
For dace are clean-shaven, like plaice.'

T. L. McCarthy

A wrestler said: 'I'm in a spot!
The pace is becoming too hot!
    My opponent's unfair –
    He's pulled out my hair,
And tied both my legs in a knot'

Frank Richards

Hall of Fame

We come to the grand and the great,
Who once guided some ship of state,
Inventors and dreamers,
The heroes and schemers,
And villains we all love to hate.

Archimedes took soap from the shell,
Then: 'You reeka!' his wife heard him yell.
    At least, that's what she thought,
    And snapped back the retort:
'You're not too bloomin' wholesome yoursel'!'
                                Douglas Catley

When thrown overboard for his crime,
Was Jonah then lost in his prime?
    No, he wasn't asleep
    In the depths of the deep,
But having a whale of a time!

C. M. M.

There was a cute fellow named Noah,
Who knew when rain came, it would pour;
    So he built a nice Ark,
    But thought it no lark,
When the elephant stuck in the door.

N. Saunders

They discovered, in Egypt, a mound
In the midst of a burial-ground;
    They were hoping like mad
    They had found Pharoah's Dad,
But his mummy was all that they found.

Frank Richards

The statuesque Queen Nefertiti
To the populace made this entreaty:
    'Those walls are specific'ly
    Carved hieroglyphic'ly,
So . . . don't muck them up with graffiti!'
Paul Alexander

Said King Arthur, that most gallant man:
'I really must draw up a plan.
    I find I'm unable
    To count round this table —
I never know where I began.'
Frank Richards

Isaac Newton, sight-seeing in Pisa,
Dropped some fruit from the Tower on a geezer;
    The man said: 'Depravity!'
    Said Newton: 'No, gravity!
But don't worry! The apple is free, sir!'
Fiona Pitt-Kethley

Said Guy Fawkes: 'I'm willing to bet
I could blow up this parliament, yet;
    The powder's all right,
    But I can't strike a light,
Because all my matches are wet.'

Frank Richards

George Stephenson said: 'These repairs
Are costing a fortune in spares.
    I'll be out of pocket
    When I've made "The Rocket",
Till British Rail raises its fares.'

Frank Richards

James Watt, one morning in spring,
Watched the kettle boil over and sing;
    He said with regret:
    'I'd invent a train yet,
If I could put wheels on the thing.'

Frank Richards

Said Wellington: 'What's the location
Of this battle I've won for the nation?'
    They replied: 'Waterloo.'
    He said: 'That'll do!
What a glorious name for a station!'

Frank Richards

'Come now,' said Bell, 'This is choice.
The first telephone! Let's rejoice!
    Now listen, folks all,
    To the very first call!'
'Sorry! Number engaged,' said a voice.

Frank Richards

Said Plimsoll: 'It's all very fine,
But the ships on the Thames and the Tyne
    Will sink without trace,
    Unless there's a place
Where someone like me draws the line.'

Frank Richards

Hans Andersen went on the spree,
And came home at a quarter past three;
    His wife, all irate,
    Screamed: 'Why are you late?
And fairy tales won't do for me!'

Frank Richards

Said Wilbur Wright: 'Oh, this is grand!
But Orville, you must understand.
    We've discovered all right
    The secret of flight –
The question is – how do we land?'

Frank Richards

'Relativity,' Einstein would say,
'Leaves no time to see you today.
    But one day I might
    Travel faster than light,
And meet you the previous day.'

P. W. R. Foot

George Washington said to his dad:
'You know that big fruit tree you had?
    I've just chopped it down.
    Now, Father, don't frown –
I can't tell a lie! Aren't you glad?'

Frank Richards

Remember the cook, Mrs Beeton,
With her book about what should be eaten?
    One day she caught 'flu,
    And fell in the stew,
So everyone's plate had more meat on.

Ann Wilde

Odd Spells

The limerick's language is queer,
As I hope to demonstrate heer.
　　The way that we write
　　May turn 'night' to 'nite'
We've such an odd language, I feer.

A small boy who lived in Iquique,
Had a voice irritatingly squique;
    When his father said: 'Oil it,
    My son, or you'll spoil it!'
His reply was a trifle too chique.

Anon.

A young English woman called St. John,
Met a red-skinned American In. John
    Who made her his bride,
    And gave her beside
A dress with a gaudy bead Frn. John.

Anon.

Said a man to his wife, down in Sydenham:
'My best trousers – where have you hydenham?
    It is perfectly true,
    They weren't very new,
But I foolishly left half a quydenham.'

P. L. Mannock

I know an old man of Durazzo.
I've never known anyone chazzo;
    From the moment he's done
    To the set of the sun,
I can only say: 'Really, is thazzo?'

Anon.

There was a young person of Bicester,
Who developed a horrible blicester;
    They said: 'When it's worse,
    We will send you a norse;
If it breaks, we will send you a sicester.'

Hic

There was a young man called Colquhoun,
Who kept, as a pet, a babuhoun;
    His mother said: 'Cholmondley!
    I don't think it quite colmondley
To feed your babuhoun with a spuhoun.'

Anon.

There once was a farmer of Biggleswade,
Who couldn't find out what his piggleswade;
    Their heads and their tails
    Went on two pairs of scails,
But he just had to guess what their miggleswade.

Mary Hayman

A venturesome three-week-old chamois
Strayed off in the woods from his mammois,
    And might have been dead,
    But some picknickers fed
Him with sandwiches, milk and salamois.

Anon.

There was a young woman of Welwyn,
Loved a barman who served at 'The Belwyn';
    But 'The Belwyn' – oh dear! –
    Had a welwyn the rear,
So they never got wed, for they felwyn.

Anon.

There was a young man of Marseilles,
Who never could master his sceilles,
    Till a girl from Bordeaux
    Showed him how they should geaux,
And he's now like a dog with two teilles.

A. C. Cossins

There was a young lady of Slough,
Who went for a ride on a cough.
    The brute pitched her off,
    When she started to coff;
She ne'er rides on such animals nough.

Langford Reed

There was a young lady called Psyche,
Who was heard to ejaculate: 'Pcryche!'
    When riding her pbych,
    She ran over a ptych,
And fell on some rails that were pspyche.

Anon.

There once was a boring old Rev.
Who preached till it seemed he would nev.
    The people and choir
    Soon started to toir,
And prayed for relief for their neth.

Anon.

A girl who weighed many an Oz.
Used language I will not pronoz.
    Her brother one day,
    Pulled her chair right away;
He wanted to see if she'd boz.

P. L. Mannock

A wandering tribe called the Siouxs
Wear moccasins, having no shiouxs.
    They are made of buckskin,
    With the fleshy side in,
Embroidered with beads of bright hiouxs.

When out on the war-path, the Siouxs
March single-file – never by tiouxs,
    And by blazing the trees
    They can return at ease,
And their way through the forest ne'er liouxs.

All new-fangled boats he eschiouxs.
And uses the birch-bark caniouxs;
    These are handy and light,
    And, inverted at night,
Give shelter from storms and from diouxs.

The principal food of the Siouxs
Is Indian maize, which they briouxs,
    And hominy make
    To mix in a cake,
Or eat it with pork as they chiouxs.

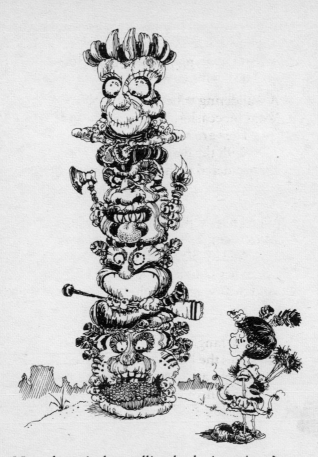

Now doesn't the spelling look ciouxrious?
'Tis enough to make anyone fiouxrious.
    So a word to the wise!
    Pray, our language revise
With orthography not so injiouxrious.

Charles Follen Adams

Puppies invariably gnaw
At items we leave on the gfloor,
    And no matter you chide them,
    The devil's inside them —
Just watch as they come back for gmore!

Tim Hopkins

Look! No Rhymes!

Some limericks choose not to rhyme
And it isn't considered a misdemeanour.
    How the words ought to be
    You just have to observe,
Though working it out may take hours, or
    even days.

There was an old man of St Bees,
Who was stung in the arm by a wasp;
    When asked: 'Does it hurt?'
    He replied: 'No, it doesn't.
Thank heavens it wasn't a hornet!'

W. S. Gilbert

There once was an elderly trout,
Who fell from a dangerous perch;
    She emitted a wail,
    And exclaimed: 'Bless my soul!
Whatever occasioned my flounder?'

H. G. B. Brown

A schoolmaster, stolid and thin
Sat down on the point of a tack;
    Though clearly designed
    To prick his esteem,
The point never entered his hide.

E. P. Stanham

There was an old man of Dunoon,
Who always ate soup with a fork;
    For he said: 'As I eat
    Neither fish, fowl, nor flesh,
I should finish my dinner too quickly.'

Anon.

There was a young fellow of Slough
Who thought he was terribly tough;
    He was set on one day
    On the banks of Newquay,
Till he shouted: 'I've had it! I'm through!'
                      H. A. C. Evans

There once was an unfortunate batsman,
Whose mother fell under the roller;
    He cried: 'All this grease
    Will ruin the pitch.
Go and fetch me a bucket of sawdust!'
                      R. S. Stanier

Twists of the Tongue

A tongue twister may twist your tongue
Till your mouth feels it's stopped by a bung;
    Your teeth and your lips
    Make terrible slips.
(The writers of these should be hung!)

There was a young fellow called Fisher,
Who was fishing for fish in a fissure,
    When a cod, with a grin,
    Pulled the fisherman in;
Now they're fishing the fissure for Fisher.

                    Anon.

A canner, exceedingly canny,
One morning remarked to his granny:
    'A canner can can
    Anything that he can,
But a canner can't can a can, can he?'

                Carolyn Wells

A tutor who taught on the flute,
Tried to teach two young tooters to toot;
    Said the two to the tutor:
    'Is it harder to toot, or
To tutor two tooters to toot?'

                    Anon.

There was a young lady of Crewe,
Who wanted to catch the 2.02;
    Said the porter: 'Don't worry,
    Or flurry, or scurry –
It's a minute or two to 2.02.'

                    Anon.

A fly and a flea in a flue
Were imprisoned, so what could they do?
    Said the fly: 'Let us flee!'
    'Let us fly!' said the flea;
So they flew through a flaw in the flue.

Anon.

There was a young person called Tate,
Who went out to dine at 8.08;
    But I will not relate
    What the person name Tate
And his *tête-à-tête* ate at 8.08.

Anon.

A keeper who worked at the zoo,
Was given a gnu to see to;
    He cried: 'That's the gnu
    That I knew at Bellevue –
I knew that I knew the new gnu.'

Frank Richards

The bottle of perfume that Willie sent
Was highly displeasing to Millicent.
    Her thanks were so cold,
    They quarrelled, I'm told,
Through the silly scent Willie sent Millicent.

Anon.

There was an old dame of Dunbar,
Who took the 4.04 to Forfar,
    But went on to Dundee,
    So she travelled, you see,
Too far by the 4.04 to Forfar.

Anon.

A right-handed fellow named Wright,
In writing 'write' always wrote 'rite'
    Where he meant to write 'write'.
    If he'd written 'write' right,
Wright would not have wrought rot writing 'rite'.

Anon.

When they catch a chinchilla in Chile,
They cut off its beard, willy-nilly,
    With a small razor blade,
    Just to say that they've made
A chinchilla's chin chilly in Chile.

                              M. C. Chandler

A teetotal chap from Dundee,
Drank half a whole bottle for tea;
    When they said that was queer,
    He replied with a leer:
'I'm not too teetotal at tea!'

                              H. J. Robinson

Glossary

A Guide to the Pronunciation of Certain Key Words in the Limericks

Beauchamp	Bee-cham
Bicester	Biss-stir
Bordeaux	Bor-doh
Chamois	Shammy
Cholmondley	Chum-ley
Colquhoun	Co-hoon
Durazzo	Doo-rats-so
Iquique	Ee-kee-kee
Marseilles	Ma-sales
Psyche	Sigh-kee
Rev.	Reverend
St. John	Singe-on
Slough	(rhymes with 'bough')
Welwyn	Well-in

Abbreviations

Cantuar:	Signature of the Archbishop of Canterbury
Cicestr:	Signature of the Bishop of Chichester
Oxon:	Signature of the Bishop of Oxford
Sarum:	Signature of the Bishop of Salisbury
Oz:	ounce

Index of Authors

Now Write Your Own Limericks
Or Collect Some New Ones from
Other People

Your Limericks

Limericks by Your Friends

New Limericks Which You Hear

Acknowledgements

I would like to express my grateful thanks to the following: Miss Joan Langford Reed for sending me some of her father's unpublished limericks; Mrs Merle Rafferty for sending me a book of unpublished limericks by her grandfather, Robert McBean Tidey; Mr William Parrott for lending me a rare volume of limericks by C. Armstrong Gibbs; Jonathan Barker, of the Arts Council Poetry Library, for assistance with research; Charles Seaton of the *Spectator* and Peter Jones of the *New Statesman* for help with limericks from their journals' literary competitions; Gabriel Rosenstock for information on the history of the limerick.

I should also like to thank the many authors who sent me their verses and the following teachers, whose pupils' work is included in this volume: Mrs K. Broomhead of Deerpark School, Wingerworth, Chesterfield; Mr N. J. Galvin of Cullingworth First School, Bradford; Ms M. Rees of Green Lane Primary School, Worcester Park; Ms R. T. James of Millway Middle School, Northampton; Miss Jane Schnapp of the Piggott School, Reading, and Mrs E. Mack of Selby High School, Selby, York; not forgetting all the other teachers and children who sent verses for me to see, most of them beautifully presented and illustrated. They gave me great pleasure and I wish I could have found room for them all.

Last but not least, my thanks to Gaby Astinax for typing the manuscript and to my wife, Tricia, without whose work and encouragement this book would never have seen the light of day.

I should like to thank the following for permission to reproduce limericks in this volume: Atheneum, New York, for limericks from *A Person from Britain* by N. M. Bodecker; BBC Publications for verses taken from *The Blue Peter Book of Limericks*, edited by Biddy Baxter and Rosemary Gill; Faber and Faber Ltd for limericks from *Verse and Worse*, edited by Arnold Silcock; Granada Publishing Ltd for various limericks from *The Lure of the Limerick* by W. Baring-Gould; Hutchinson Publishing Group Ltd for limericks from *The Beaver Book of Revolting Rhymes*, edited by Jennifer and Graham Curry and *Versicles and Limericks*, edited by Charles Connell; Michael Joseph Ltd for verses from *The Best and Only 101 Limericks of Spike Milligan* by Spike Milligan, published by Michael Joseph with M. & J. Hobbs; Gershon Legman and Kryptádia Inc. for limericks from *The Limerick*, published by Jupiter Books, London, and *The New Limerick*, published by Crown Publishers Inc., New York, both edited by Gershon Legman; Methuen & Co. Ltd for limericks from *The Everyman Century of Humorous Verse*, edited by Roger Lancelyn Green, published by J. M. Dent & Sons Ltd; Pan Books for limericks from *The Pan Book of Limericks*, edited by Untermeyer; Penguin Books Ltd for limericks from *More Comic and Curious Verse* and *Yet More Comic and Curious Verse*, edited by J. M. Cohen; G. P. Putnam's Sons, New York, for verses from *Spilt Milk* by Morris Bishop, copyright © 1942 by Morris Bishop, renewed 1969; The *Daily Mail* for a limerick by M. C. Chandler; the *New Statesman* and the *Spectator* for limericks taken from their literary competitions, including one by J. Michie; and *Punch* for 'There was an old man of Dunoon' (1920).

I am also indebted to the Estate of Conrad Aiken for limericks by Conrad Aiken from *A Seizure of Limericks*, published by W. H. Allen & Co. Ltd; Cyril Bibby for limericks from his book *The Art of the Limerick*, published by the Research Publishing Co.; Mrs Douglas Catley of Cape Catley Ltd for limericks from *A Dabble of Limericks* by the late Douglas Catley; Atheneum, New York, and Edward Gorey for limericks taken from his book *The Listing Attic*; Jean Harrowven for limericks by N. Saunders, Carl Stevenson and C. K. Thomson, and four anonymous limericks from her book *The Limerick Makers*, published by the Research Publishing Co. and Ann Robinson and the directors of the Cheltenham Festival for a limerick by H. J. Robinson.

All limericks by Langford Reed by kind permission of Joan Langford Reed, also the verses taken from *The Complete Limerick Book*: those by P. L. Mannock, Dixon Merritt, Cosmo Monkhouse, George Robey and F. J. Smith, and the following anonymous limericks: 'There was a young lady of Lynn' (p. 17); 'There was an old fellow of Tyrc' (p. 22); 'An old man who sat on the front' (p. 25); 'There was an old man of the Nore,' (p. 29); 'There was a young seedsman of Leeds,' (p. 44); 'There was a young lady of Tottenham,' (p. 59); 'We thought him an absolute lamb,' (p. 60); 'There was an old hag of Malacca,' (p. 67); 'There was an old man of Peru,' 'There was a young lady of Twickenham' (p. 69); 'There was a young girl of Asturias,' (p. 75); 'There was a young lady called Perkins,' (p. 83); 'An epicure, dining at Crewe,' (p. 85); 'A barber who lived in Batavia' (p. 95); 'A tiger with tastes anthropophagous,' (p. 98); 'There once was a Plesiosaurus,' (p. 99); 'A small boy who lived in Iquique,' (p. 116); 'I know an old man of Durazzo.' (p. 116); 'There was a young woman of Welwyn,' (p. 118); 'There was a young lady called Psyche,' (p. 119); 'There was a young fellow called Fisher,', 'A tutor who taught on the flute,', 'There was a young lady of Crewe,' (p. 127); 'A fly and a flea in a flue', 'There was a young person called Tate,' (p. 128); 'The bottle of perfume that Willie sent', 'There was an old dame of Dunbar,', 'A right-handed fellow named Wright,' (p. 129).

Last, but not least, I am grateful to the following for permission to include limericks in this volume: Paul Alexander, Peter Alexander, Lorna Bain, William Bealby-Wright, Alan Clark, Wendy Cope, Coral Copping, A. P. Cox, Susan Emanuel, Michelle Games, Robert Gray, Bill Greenwell, Paul Griffin, Gerry Hamill, Mary Hayman, Richard Heller, Mary Holtby, Tim Hopkins, Joyce Johnson for her own limericks and one by Leslie Johnson, C.M.M., Harriet Mandelbaum, T. L. McCarthy, Thomas McDonald, George McWilliam, Rachel Moore, Betty Morris, Cyril Mountjoy, Vincent Mulholland, Fiona Pitt-Kethley, Val Pöhler, A. G. Prys-Jones, Frank Richards, B. Ridley, Ron Rubin, G. B. Scott, Ruth Silcock, Ida Thurtle, Bland Tomkinson, W. F. N. Watson, Ann Wilde and David Woodsford.

Every effort has been made to trace copyright holders. We would be grateful to hear from any copyright holders not here acknowledged.